When Y

MW01042450

A book of inspiration, poetry and lessons learned
from a battle with cancer

by
Leslie Droll

Published by Droll Enterprises
Fostoria, Ohio

ISBN 0-9720263-0-4
LCCN 2002091734

Printed in U.S. by The Gray Printing Company

FOREWORD

This collection of poems and stories are expressions of my journey through life. As a cancer survivor, I have witnessed cancer from the perspective of a daughter, wife, mother, sister, aunt, cousin, friend, and co-worker.

As a child, I experienced my father dying of cancer. My mother is a colon cancer survivor (still bowling games over 200 at age 85!). As an adult, I lost my older sister, Phyllis, to lung cancer. Recently, my eldest daughter Dana (now 22 years young) was diagnosed with malignant melanoma. I am a breast cancer survivor.

My family shares a sucky gene pool that would seem to make us pre-disposed to developing cancer. I have accepted this, but I believe there is much more to cancer than simply heredity. I have researched the medical, physical, psychological, and spiritual aspects of dealing with cancer. *Cancer* is my nemesis, and I am *The Cancer Vigilante*.

I became a volunteer patient advocate, and began to speak to anyone who wanted to communicate with a cancer survivor. I championed a support group called "The Lunch Bunch", since that is what we are: A group of people "out to lunch". ☺ (I love you guys!)

3

In June of 1999, my husband noticed a "For Sale" sign in a yard with a river view, as he was fishing from our jet ski. The Maumee River had been our weekend retreat for over twenty years; our favorite place on earth to camp, fish, or just relax. Since my illness, we had begun taking life, literally, "one day to the next" ~ enjoying every waking moment.

In October of 1999, we chose to *move* to that beautiful home on the riverfront, surrounded by nature. This would be the beginning of our "simulated retirement". Our beautiful, peaceful retreat lay 'across the river and through the woods' near Grand Rapids, Ohio. Our home is nestled on three acres surrounded by woods, and fronted by the river. We knew our "permanent guests" would include Wally the one-eyed poodle, Tom the cat, and Itty-Bitty (the runt of a litter of kittens that Dana rescued) who thinks he is a lion.

Now, we have a one-hour drive (each way) to work. It actually seems more like a blessing than a strain ~ to ride in the car together for two hours each weekday. For most married couples, such time is wasted. To us, it's time together...*finally*. We realize now, that every moment of each day - from the commute to our work places to each sunrise and sunset - should be observed and absorbed...like nutrition for your soul.

This book has been in my head for some time, and it is time to let it out! I hope that you have found this book because you are - as I was - in need of hope, and seeking inspiration.

4

<u>When You Get It</u> is a paradox. When you get "it" (cancer, another illness, loss of a loved one, or any other life-altering experience), you begin to ***get it***. Life takes on new meaning, respect, and responsibility. That compelling revelation has been the driving force behind this book. It is written in the hope that the expression of my experience will help others find *their* peace on earth.

This book is dedicated to

Mike, Dana, and Angie
Mom and Dad
Phyllis, Kathy, and Jim
Kent,
Laurie Leigh,
Teresa, Sarah &
Linda,
and all of those remarkable people
who have loved me and supported me
forever.

Acknowledgments

This book is a true labor of love. Without the support of so many people, this would have surely remained a dream. Special thanks go to Mike Droll for his great ideas, love and inspiration; Kent Babb of Babb-O-Rama (www.babborama.com) for Web design, nomination for the Olympic Torch, as well as book development & design; Dana Droll for emotional and inspirational support; Angie Dessausure for logo design; Laurie Leigh Keller for copyediting & good karma; Linda Woodland for her Lambscape and inspiration; Sarah McClelland and Theresa Margraf, for their stories; Photo Smith, Wayne, Ohio, for photo reprints; the Review Times, Fostoria, Ohio, for reprint; and Quality Press.

I would also like to acknowledge the communities of Fostoria, Findlay, Grand Rapids, and Liberty Center, Ohio - the places we've called home over the years, and the special people who have supported our business ventures, renewed my health, and helped us raise our children.

Table of Contents

On Surviving
Beginning or End?
Fear
Hole Through Your Soul
Extra Credit

On Finding Peace
The River
Along the Way
Angels
Sunset Observed
Be Yourself
Leave a Mark

My Life/My Movie
The Torch ~ Run for Your Life
Sarah
My Third Grader
Skippyville
My Girls
My Way
Winter
Tree Farmers
The Crossing Guard
Love, Medicine, & Miracles
Linda's Miracle
Lambscapes
Quality as Life
Being Bald

For Fun
Toast
The Scrapbook
Parent
When You Get It
My Body, My Car
California
Red Hair
Jealousy
Living on a Boat
The Garden
If I Could Fly
Turtles
On the Dock
Seasons
When They Tell You

On Surviving

This chapter contains my thoughts regarding survival, and how it can be accomplished day-by-day.

My definition of a "survivor" is anyone who has been faced with mortality - their own, or that of another. We will all experience this one day.

Therefore, if you are reading this book, *you are a survivor*.

Beginning or End?

You have CANCER They've told you
Eyes fill with tears
A day to remember
Can't control the fear

You cry for the first day
But, then you must pledge
To determine the meaning
New Beginning? Or End?

Choose *New Beginning*!
Life's "second chance"
Muster your courage
With no backward glance

God, family, vacation ~
Your new lease on life
Forgetting the everyday
Struggles and strife

Cut, burn, or poison?
Must you pursue treatment?
Not glamorous choices
But, life's bittersweet-ness

A vow of survival
A mission plan set
Surgery, radiation, or chemo?
How bad can it get?

You give up some flesh
Take poison ~ how bold
Irradiate your skin to 100 years old

Some go bald in the process
And needles abound
It's hard to believe
That you're not losing ground

Then, there are the people
You've met on the way
Be thankful for them
Each and every day

Not due to the illness
But the lessons it brought
Trade in this journey?
I would guess not

Without this experience
How would you know
What courage you have
Or how far you could go?

To get one more chance
At the legacy you'd leave...
You couldn't imagine
What God had up His sleeve!

For cancer has taught me
To give God His due
And pass on this message
From me to you

Believe in the miracles
While working to come back
God ~ and the angels
Will keep you on track!

Fear

Have you ever been scared
By the voice in your head?
Can you make it stop?
Does it cause you dread?

Fear is a demon
It preys on your mind
No more powerful feeling
On earth will you find

This emotion can harm you
Just realize
It is an *emotion* ~
Not justified!

We can free our spirit
From this painful grip
That takes hold of our heart strings
And just will not quit

So the next time it visits
(This *Fear* in your life)
Release your emotion!
Let go of the strife!

Your body is able
Your mind, it is free
Your spirit can choose
Tranquility

Hole Through Your Soul

How did it get there ~
That hole through your soul?
Do you know when it happened?
Did it *feel* like a hole?

It comes as a crisis
A change in your life
It may be camouflaged
In trouble and strife

Sometimes it's a job
Or a loss, such as death
A loved one so precious...
You can't catch your breath

Your heart may seem broken
Or maybe your head
Making you feel crazy
Filling your life with dread

But deep in your body
It opens a hole
Allowing disease
That weakens your soul

Did you give up on life?
Were you out of control?
Did you cry in your sleep?
Could you crawl in a hole?

Did you get angry?
Were you real sad?
Did you lose the best friend
That you ever had?

Don't let it take over!
Fight the good fight!
Love is the bandage
To cover this site.

Extra Credit

If illness comes early
Life takes new form
Aware of mortality
Change from the norm

I've experienced 80
At 40 years old
Cancer, the courier.
Risks ~ they were bold.

Precious life threatened
I sensed a new cause
To listen more closely
To life's silent pause

So much to absorb!
Life moves on so quick!
Why must we suffer?
Why be *so sick*?

Now we must ponder
Our visit on earth ~
The journey beginning
The day of our birth

I will make the best
Of each brand new day
Even the ones
That "don't go my way"...

For every chance
That I have to **get it**
While remaining on earth
Must be *extra credit*!

On Finding Peace

It is important for every human being to find personal peace: A quiet place, your personal definition of God, or your purpose on the planet. I don't know if my personal peace comes from within. But, I do know that if I feed it by helping others ~ or just listening ~ it makes things better.

The River

The place of my childhood
A liquid oasis
A dream...a picture
My favorite of places

One hour from home
Each Friday we sought
The kids and the dog ~
What an exciting thought!

We're seeking FAMILY
Finding free time!
We could not imagine
The marvelous find

For joy and for freedom ~
Our place in the sun
A real morale-booster
Reservation for fun!

Along the Way

You were a child
So full of love
That could not be defined ~
It came from Above!

And as you grew wiser
All along the way
There were so many outlets
To love and to pray

Love is the answer
To so many things...
Joy, peace, and grace
Let you hear your heart sing

Just keep passing love on!
In the moment it takes
You cannot imagine
The difference it makes!

Yet, along the way
Let us not forget
The Lord has requested
We have no regret

So, if you've a gift
Down deep in your heart
It's *never* too late
To make a new start

Along the way
Take time to share
Tell someone you meet
That you really *do* care

You can make a difference
Just by what you say
In some kind words of love
Shared with others each day

Angels

They are among us
Friends from the past
Not yet reunited
Yet, together ~ at last

We miss them quite often
But the loneliness wanes
Until you hear whispers
From *Memory Lane*

A song that you hear
Quotes from a book
Someone says something ~
You give them a look

The voice of your conscience?
A coincidence, right?
Or was it a dream
That you had in the night?

Has this ever happened
To you, or a friend?
Have you been told a story
And *known* the end?

I believe in angels ~
The Spirit of Hope
They've sustained my composure
Helping me cope

The most beautiful image ~
A glory with wings
Ebony or Ivory
The *Spirit* of things

23

24

Sunset Observed

Have you ever stood silent
Before the night fall
Facing the west
Hearing birds call?

No matter your location
It is always there
Right at the tree line
For you to share

No need for investment
In travel afar
To witness God's beauty ~
He's given us stars!

An evening adventure
To witness the sun
Setting at dusk
On the horizon

They change with the seasons,
Locations, and colors...
With deep orange and blue
Unlike any other

Clouds add dimension.
Rain blocks it out.
Yet, it's there every evening
Without a doubt!

A perfect dessert
To end every day...
You've only to look,
To thank God, and pray.

Any Situation Life Throws Your Way Can Be Handled With Quality

A letter to the editor of Quality Press, October, 1997

Brad Stratton's article "Quality as a Way of Life" (July 1997, p. 28) definitely struck a chord with me. I am the quality manager at Kenhar Dyson in Findlay, OH, a leading manufacturer of forks for the material handling industry.

My story begins on Friday, Oct. 13, 1995, when I was diagnosed with breast cancer at age 42. I initially reacted as anyone would – tears, pain, anger, and, above all, fear. After giving myself a few hours to stabilize my emotions, I sat down to rationalize a plan. Since quality systems are my life and I tend to use my expertise to examine and define goals in all aspects of my life, I didn't think that I should treat cancer any differently.

I now know that this approach might have helped to save my life, as well as eased the burden on my family. I had contemplated this plan while awaiting my diagnosis so I would have something to fall back on if the prognosis was cancer. Since it was, I then began to implement the plan. I first spoke to each family member – my husband and two teen-age daughters – individually and shared my plan. First, we were each allowed a day to vent our anger in any appropriate way other than hitting the dog or each other. This gave us a release to enable each of us to better deal with the next phase.

26

The following day I prepared for another surgery, but my daughters preferred to remain in school and continue with their normal routines. I helped my daughters by sending their principal a note explaining my plight and asking him to inform all of their teachers so they would understand any moments of panic. Later, I returned to their school during chemotherapy treatments, when I was bald, to share my story about living throughout this ordeal.

I fully believe that my systems allowed me to approach cancer treatment with a positive attitude and to cope through very difficult decisions. For example, when I was told that all of my waist-length hair would fall out, instead of thinking about it negatively, I saw it as a chance to see myself as a new person, without the image that I had created with hair. Many of us relate to a person by their outward appearance, and I found it refreshing to sport a bald head. In fact, I found that people who spoke to me were more intimidated to speak to me, than I was speaking to them. I believe this is because everyone fears the disease, and they must meet their fears head-on when they meet a bald person with cancer.

I also studied mental imagery while taking chemotherapy. I would wear headphones to treatment and listen to soft music or to books on tape to mentally remove myself from the treatment. I only became nauseated once and did not experience many negative side effects. In fact, I even visited a tanning booth when I was in treatment and bald, to make myself look healthier on the exterior to help my self-esteem. I was especially happy when people would say "you look great" and comment on my healthy complexion and outlook.

My system included many quality disciplines that I have learned in my profession:

Corrective action. I have the disease now and must plan my treatment and follow it through.

Preventive action. I changed my eating habits and diet to a more acceptable system to help me retain the energy I needed to endure chemotherapy, as well as improve my future chances of good health.

Forward planning. I read every book the library could offer, searched the Internet, and visited the American Cancer Society and the local United Way agencies. I also attended the "I Can Cope" program three times, an informative program sponsored by the American Cancer Society at my local hospital.

I had family pictures, as well as individual pictures taken while I still had long hair. I then had another picture taken when I was bald to use as evidence when I am 80 and telling my grandchildren this story.

Strategic planning. I met with many other cancer patients, physicians, and support people that helped me become better educated about my disease. I met with my lawyer and assigned a power of attorney, drew up a living will, and put all legal issues in order. This gave my family some sense of security, and I was able to make some of my own decisions about my care and future. When my hair began to fall out, my family shaved off the rest at my request, so I was in charge of losing my hair, not the cancer.

Cancer makes you feel out of control, and knowing what I know about quality, I was sure I could organize this situation and get my life back into control. Throughout the past two years, I have truly

28

grown to be a better human being because of this experience. Both personally and professionally, I have a wealth of knowledge about the importance of life and living it to the fullest. My priorities are not the same as before. Before, my priorities were family, money, profession and God. Now they are God, family, ice cream, and vacation.

Life is grand! With the right plan, I believe you can take back control of your life in any unusual circumstance. You cannot guarantee a complete success, but you can get better mileage out of the life you lead.

Leslie Droll, Kenhar Dyson Inc.
Findlay, OH

Be Yourself

When you are in trouble,
Find yourself.
When you are older,
Be yourself.

Fear of the future ~
See yourself.
Questions unanswered?
Trust yourself.

Always prepare
To know yourself.
Whenever you're challenged,
Just *be yourself.*

Who do you know best?
Your *Self.*
Love gives you courage ~
Love being yourself.

Great happiness comes
From who you are.
It takes honest acceptance
To love yourself.

Leave a Mark

You're given *one chance*
For a memory to leave
Upon this, your planet,
If you believe.

We each have a mission ~
Do you know your part?
Have you made a difference?
Or, is *this* the start?

When you were a child
What did you like?
Have you followed your dream?
Or, is this your plight ~

To exist without *mission*
Would be a great loss
To this earthly vision...
The ultimate cost.

Don't live life "on empty"
Not filling your cup
Now, come ~ get ready!
You just have to stand up

For what you believe in!
That's all that it takes!
Leave a mark on the planet
With the difference you make.

"Being" is important,
tell people your story

My Life/My Movie

When I write of my life, I share my experience and wit in short poems and stories. This is "my movie" ~ and I felt I should share some important events to help you get to know me.

Former Fostorian gets Olympic flame

102-year-old torchbearer passes flame on to Droll
by Brad Johnson
Staff Writer
From the Fostoria (Ohio) Review-Times – January 4, 2002
Reprinted with permission

"I had the time of my life," former-Fostorian Leslie Droll said of her Olympic Torchbearing experience Thursday morning at Moraine, a suburb of Dayton.

Droll, a cancer survivor, was selected to carry the Olympic Torch for the 2002 Olympic Games in Salt Lake City, Utah after being nominated by her older sister's son, Kent Babb.

Sarah McClelland of Xenia, the oldest torchbearer in the 2002 Olympic Torch Relay at 102-years-old, handed off to Droll on Dorothy Lane at approximately 10:30 a.m. McClelland, who broke her hip in four places in September, began carrying the torch in a wheelchair, but got up and used a walker for the last half of the .2 of a mile, according to www.saltlake2002.com.

Droll and her husband Mike, moved from Fostoria to Liberty Center two years ago, but still own and operate Droll Refrigeration Service in Fostoria.

As her sister was claimed by cancer, Droll used her own experience to help the family through the ordeal, giving Babb the idea to nominate his aunt this past spring when a friend told him about the opportunity.

34

"The day before Thanksgiving we found out that my oldest daughter, Dana (22 yrs. old) had malignant melanoma, a very serious form of skin cancer," Droll said. "So needless to say I have another reason to run. She is fine and her prognosis is very good, but that word CANCER never makes it easy."

Of the 210,000 nominees, 7,200 were chosen to carry the torch on its 13,500 mile journey from Atlanta, the most recent site of the Olympic Games in the United States, to Salt Lake City.

The Torch ~ Run for Your Life

The *Olympic Torch*
An honor to touch
To carry this icon
Would mean so much

Nominations requested
And then came the date
That an e-mail announced
I'd participate!

Of 210,000
My story stood out!
One of 7,200
In the final count

Once in a lifetime
Came following a fear
Recalling the reason
Brought on a tear

So many losses!
The illness ~ so real.
Emotions are streaming...
I must make an appeal

My real-life experience
The lessons it's taught
Cancer *cannot* win
This battle long-fought

A father, a mother,
a sister, and I.
Now, even my daughter ~
Why *her*, too? *Why?*

This run is an honor
A symbol, for me
A light carried far
Through the land of the free

This run is for *life*!
I can use it to show
Millions of people
That cancer must *GO*!

January 3, 2002 – 102-year-old Sarah McClellen (left) passes
the Olympic flame to me.
(I'm the white blob on the right!)

39

Sarah

She is Sarah McClellan
One hundred and two
"She's part of a family
That is one of so few

Who have lived three centuries
In Xenia, Ohio",
The news had reported
In her *Torch Bearer* bio

To pass on the flame
For 2002
Is an Olympic epic
Awarded to few...

My nephew Kent's essay
Would nominate me
He gave me the nickname
Cancer Vigilante!

To meet Sarah was special!
She carried the torch
Along Dorothy Lane
Past someone's front porch

How was I involved?
Just what was my duty?
To receive the fire
From this awesome cutie!

Sarah was amazing!
I was inspired
By the quiet lady
Who never grew tired

My life has been changed
By this event
Because I know it was
A *true* gift ~ Heaven sent!

My third grader (and friends)

42

My Third Grader

Boys have a talent ~
A way to stay young...
Collecting their toys
Has only begun

When you marry a young man
You think he is grown
Until you uncover
"*The Kid*"~ with a moan

He's not really hiding
He's always there
Behind the exterior
Is a third grader...Beware!

The life of a child
Is first in their mind
A land of adventure
Left not far behind

Youthful forever!
Make no mistake ~
If he acts any different
It must be a fake

A man on the outside
So strong and so sure
But way down beneath
Is a youth that endures

Imagine the happiness
The world would see
If the old would stay young!
How *fun* that would be!

The future's our choice...
This could be the answer!
A solution for old age?
A cure for cancer?

Laughing and playing
A wonderful life
A world overflowing
No trouble or strife

So, next time he appears
(The third grader beneath)
Don't scold him away
He's wise beyond belief!

Sunset in Skippyville

Skippyville

We traveled by water
Upon a jet ski
Arriving ashore
Our new home to see

Where was this new land?
Was this a dream?
We followed our hearts
Across river and stream

We crossed over the river
Traveled through the woods
In front of this bungalow
The two of us stood

A change in our outlook ~

45

A different view
Such risks in a lifetime
Would be taken by few

It gives us such peace~
A feeling of ease
Surrounded by nature
And God, we are pleased

Skip is our neighbor ~
The first to appear
Introducing himself
As he welcomed us here

"He must be the Mayor!"
Mike soon surmised
So we call our town *Skippyville*...
Our life of surprise!

A new life together....
Leaving the nest
Moving to *Skippyville*...
To live in the Forest.

Sisters' birth mark events in hostage crisis

By Denise Sakal
City Editor

From the Fostoria (Ohio) Review-Times – January 22, 1981
Reprinted with permission

The hostage crisis is an historical event that will be long remembered – especially for Michael and Leslie Droll of Fostoria

On Nov. 4, 1979, militants seized the American embassy in Iran, and Mrs. Droll gave birth to the couple's first child, Dana.

After 444 days of captivity, the 52 American hostages were freed…and Mrs. Droll gave birth to their second daughter, Angela.

The seven pound, five ounce baby girl was born at 9:07 p.m. Tuesday at Fostoria City Hospital, 12 days later than expected. The birth follows the prediction of the couple's niece who said Sunday the baby would not be born until the hostages were released.

Ironically, Mrs. Droll said she felt fine Tuesday morning and didn't expect to give birth that day.

Her labor pains began at 11 a.m. shortly after she heard the hostages had been released.

She gave birth to her first baby 24 days later than expected, after having been in labor for 30 hours.

Mrs. Droll said "it's an odd coincidence" and admitted to being preoccupied with searching for a meaning behind the events.

"Maybe there's nothing to it, maybe there

47

was," she said with a smile. "It makes me wonder if someday it's going to all come together."

The event means nothing to the girls now, but Mrs. Droll said she'll save the newspapers marking the beginning and end of the crisis.

"I don't know how important it'll (their births) be in history, or how unimportant. But, I'm sure they'll think about it," she added.

When asked whether they plan to have other children, the couple gave a harmonious smile, and an agreeable nod.

The family resides at 218 Elwood Ave.

My Girls

The first is named Dana ~
She's her Dad's biggest fan!
Born when the hostages
Were seized in Iran.

The second is Angela~
Born in 1/81
As release of the hostages
Had just begun.

Corresponding events
Coincidental, we ask?
Yet even *more* parallels
Would soon come to pass…

444 days,
One birth to the other~
444 is our business address
So notes my mother!

Dana's birth shared the
Election Day date.
How could Angie's birthday
Ever relate?

When Angie was born
That day in "81
Reagan's *inauguration*
Had just begun!

Dana's blonde with blue eyes
Angie? Brown-eyed brunette
Two ends of the spectrum
Yet, they match like a set.

How will their unique
Life stories unfold?
I will enjoy telling it~
When I am old.

My Way

Living life is an art
My way to be bold
I follow my heart
With the hope to grow old

There is no right way
Better than the others
If you follow the rules
Loving your brother

Freedom is the key
Hope unrelenting
Inner voice essential
Rhythm consenting

Nature the breath
Peace of heart
Dreams of promise
Until we must part

Belief everlasting
Time must be savored
Pleasure enjoyed
Life so full of flavor

Winter

Shimmering beauty
Silent of sound
Crisp and cold
Frozen ground

Winter's blanket of snow
Awaits springtime's rebirth
Each season's a miracle
Here on this earth

Resting ~ reflecting
Energy renewal
Provides for future
Summer fuel

Trees are barren
Garden at rest
Winter's white palette
We thank God ~ we're so blessed

Tree Farmers

Once upon a time
I had a thought...
We could raise trees
For the oxygen they brought

Can you imagine
A better profession
Than watching trees grow?
(That's my confession)

Nut trees and conifers
Hardwoods and fruit
Willows and shrubs
Grown to suit

So many to choose from ~
Walnuts to Birch
A refuge where song birds
Can rest and perch

A forest for profit
An enchanted wood
Giving air to breathe freely ~
Oh my! Life is good!

The Crossing Guard

She was there every day. A very pleasant looking lady. I would pass her, in my car, at the intersection in front of the rural school. Once I had returned to work - following eight months of cancer treatment - I began to take notice. She was bold. She would often wave her red hand-held stop sign at the semi-trucks, indicating to them that they should slow down.

This particular morning, it was cold and raining. Although I was warm and dry inside my car, I began allowing the feeling of depression to seep into my head. When I was diagnosed with cancer, I made a promise to myself to *pay attention* to life, and to acknowledge others who seemed to take pride in their own lives. I had vowed to not allow myself to waste one moment thinking negative thoughts.

As I approached the school, the guard motioned for me to stop. As I did, I observed this lady in rain gear ~ with an umbrella that covered her *and* several small children ~ crossing the street. It was a drenching rain, yet the guard was smiling! Under her guidance, the children appeared to be oblivious to the rain and the dangers of crossing the street. The umbrella was made of a clear material, and was shaped like a bunny head ~ complete with eyes and ears.

The crossing guard made me think of a mother duck with her small ducklings. The sight made me feel warm, made me smile, and above all, shook me out of the "funk" that I had been in just the moment before. I proceeded to work, and immediately composed a

55

note to the crossing guard. I mailed it to her, in care of the rural school.

In the note, I explained to this special lady what an impression she had made upon me that morning. I told her how I had surmised that she must care a great deal about her job - and her young charges - by the enjoyment that shone on her face. As I mailed the card, I had a sense that I had crossed a threshold in my new awakening by acknowledging this soul in such a personal way.

Several days later, a card arrived in *my* mail. The return address was unfamiliar. As I opened it, I knew it was a special card. It was shaped like an angel. I sensed that something remarkable had taken place. You see, the card was from the crossing guard ~ in response to my note.

She explained that sometimes people must think that she is "way too serious" about her job. However, she went on to reveal that when she was thirteen years old ~ attending that same rural school along with her seven year old sister ~ her sister was struck and killed in that very intersection. That day, she vowed to protect the children of the school.

The pact I had made with my spirit had paid off. An *awareness*, sparked by a common event, had allowed me to change the direction of my life! I think that by sharing my *response* to that moment with the crossing guard, I may have made a difference in her life, too.

Love, Medicine, & Miracles

I had been in treatment for breast cancer. One afternoon my doorbell rang. At the door, I met Linda ~ the daughter of a former co-worker. I was surprised to see Linda; and even more surprised when she handed me a book. It was a copy of Love, Medicine, & Miracles, written by Dr. Bernie Siegel. Linda was in the throes of a battle with a neurological condition when her mother, Lillian, had given her the book. Linda's story was so remarkable, that it was obviously nothing short of a miracle that she recovered.

I was deeply touched by the knowledge that I had a friend who cared enough to want me to experience the book, that she had personally delivered it to me. It was so moving to know that a book so close to my beliefs even *existed*. I immediately read the book from cover-to-cover.

The following summer, some time after I received the book, my husband and I were about to embark on a tandem bicycle ride. I suddenly remembered the book, and asked Mike if he would mind stopping at Lillian's house to return it. I would enjoy seeing Linda and Lillian again.

Mike owns and operates a heating and air conditioning service business. I did not know that my friends had been clients of his for several years. He thought paying them a visit was an excellent idea ~ he could also check their furnace and air conditioner while we were there! When we arrived, Lillian was standing at the front door of the house, as if she had been expecting me. She opened the door and exclaimed, "I *knew* God would answer my prayer! I'm *so* glad you've come!"

Lillian gave me a hug, and asked me to come in and help her talk to her daughter, Linda. I had been unaware that my friend was so ill. Lillian was wearing an oxygen hook-up. They had just returned from a visit to the physician. The prognosis was grim. Lillian had only a very short time left to live. The arthritis she suffered from had damaged her lungs beyond repair. Due to her age, she was not a candidate for a transplant.

Linda was trying to sort this all out. She wanted desperately to find another option, so that her mother might live awhile longer. They were very close. They shared a home and a daily life together. Like any other child, Linda was not ready to lose her mother. Lillian, however, was preparing for her next journey - to heaven - and she wanted very badly to get consent from Linda for that passage. This day would also be an epiphany to me, because Lillian was asking *me* to help her get her daughter's approval to leave her loved ones and move on to a higher place. Although I had gone through that same thought process in dealing with my cancer ~ wondering how I would talk to *my* two daughters if I were forced to face an untimely death ~ I was still a little unsettled by Lillian's request. I had no idea what was about to take place.

I did not have time to think about it a great deal, yet the answer seemed to be right in my hand. I held out Dr. Siegel's book to Linda, and suggested that maybe

58

I had been *sent* to return it to her. Reading it again would allow her to recall the valuable lessons it provided. We all laughed. We all cried. I believe that there was a Higher Power at work that day, and I was merely the vehicle by which the message was to be delivered.

My dear friend Lillian died two days after this meeting.

Lillian had encouraged my friendship with Linda, and I dearly cherish our connection. Linda says, "There is nothing like the love of a mother for healing her child

Linda's Miracle

Lillian's daughter, Linda, had a neurological condition. The disease had ravaged her body, leaving her paralyzed. Miraculously, she regained all of her physical abilities in a long, relentless fight against all odds

I first saw Linda's paintings when I visited her home to return the book, <u>Love, Medicine, and Miracles</u>. Her paintings - vibrantly colored landscapes painted in oil on canvas that include one or more little lambs in the background - are extraordinary.

Linda's paintings are called *lambscapes*, because they depict remarkable landscapes that are accented with lovely little lambs.

Linda's paintings are inspirational and uplifting. You sense that they are a glimpse of the Divine ~ as if her hands were guided in their creation by The Creator, Himself.

One of Linda's Lambscapes

Lambscapes

Have you ever been witness
To an image from God?
A picture, a painting
Mostly of sod?

Then you've not seen a "Lambscape"
The green is so pure
The lambs are quit precious
Of this I am *sure*.

I stood in a daydream~
Looking *inside*
Beyond the colored canvas
Of this work done with pride

They each tell a story
The lamb *Oh so wise*
The color enthralls you
Cannot move your eyes

For never before
Has God taken a hand
Then added the paint
Changing canvas to land

You see in the lamb
A small quiet soul
That speaks in such volumes
Of God's healing goals

Quality As Life

If you have been to that place inside yourself that allows you to reflect upon your contribution to this life, you will realize that you have been influenced ~ and continue to be influenced every day ~ by symbols, messages, and subtle signs from heaven.

I believe in taking responsibility for my own actions. Your *reaction* to forces that are beset upon you is ultimately what shapes your destiny. Life can be so full and powerful if you *invest* in your journey. Every day provides you with a new opportunity to react to, and reflect upon. If we expect everything in life to happen without any responsibility or investment on our part, it will be a hollow journey.

Challenge is a force that inspires *reaction*. If a person holds true to their values and beliefs as they face life's challenges, the outcome can be magical. *Fulfillment* is achieved when we accept responsibility for our active participation in the events of the day. We must **make** life happen...not just wait around for the experience to happen to us.

Before…

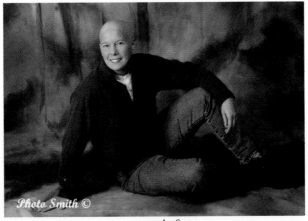

…and after

Being Bald

I chose chemo
"You'll lose your hair,"
The doctor said.
I didn't care.

"Will I still need
To shave my legs?"
He stared back with
A solemn face.

(Seemed like a normal
question to me!)

Well I *cannot*
Give up my hair!
(Even though I said
I didn't care...)

On a journey
We would go.
How it would feel
We did not know.

But, my family
Would take it off ~
The entire length...
Long and soft.

We'd video tape
The "Shave of Life"
To help us all
Cope with the strife.

My oldest girl
Would do the shave.
(A little hair
We'll have to save.)

She took a swipe
Across the top
Soon she'd removed
The entire crop.

And, now I'm bald.
"What a nice round head!"
Were the first words that
My husband said.

But, all in all,
A small price to pay...
I **loved** being bald
Is all I will say!

For Fun

This chapter is meant to make you smile, and to just give you something to think about.

Toast

Something with crust
Cooked until brown
Are you thinking "food"?
Turn that thought around

What if the topic
To which this applied
Was to a *person*
Who has been "fried"?

It happens to people
As well as to food
"Toast" is descriptive
Hard to elude

For those who have earned it~
The title of "Toast" ~
Their *brain* is the thing
They have damaged the most.

You get just one body
So do not forget
To treat it with kindness~
Life's not over yet!

Maybe you've not listened
Or you've ignored the signs
Abusive mistreatment
Of your body ~ your mind

Then *you* may be "Toast"
The word would apply
To your very life
From which you can't hide

The Scrapbook

A loving gesture
Paper and glue
A card in the mailbox
Sent just for you

Someone loves you dearly
Or sends you a laugh
Held in your fingers
Love in your grasp

So inexpensive
This symbol of hope
A card can be magic
Helping you cope

A message so tender
It could make you cry
You don't have to answer
Or give a reply

You can read it over
Again and again
A lovely reminder
That you have a friend

Hallmark greetings
Forever to keep
They're kept in a scrapbook
No matter how cheap

A book full of paper
Some stamps and some glue
Who could have imagined
The joy it brings you?

Parent

They arrive on the planet
Naked and scared
Smiles await them ~
People who care

Love like no other
Parents give; no regrets
The job of a lifetime
With no "safety nets"

This job is an honor
Not an "auto entitle"
Life changes so quickly
No more sitting idle

First steps, First words,
First day of school,
First date, First kiss,
Living the Golden Rule

Healer, Counselor,
Financial Advisor,
Judge, Taxi Driver,
Always getting wiser

All children are blessings
They're God's greatest gift
To love and to nurture
To guide and uplift

And when you grow old
You hope they'll show others
Love, faith, hope, and kindness
When *they're* fathers and mothers

When You Get It

Life is decisions
Listen to soul
Understanding each moment
God is in control

Hearing your calling
Taking stock
Paying attention
Careful talk

Listening contently
Giving back
Having great patience
Staying on track

Giving credit to Him
Strength in time of need
Love unconditional
The will to succeed

When you finally *get it*
Life becomes calm
Grateful tolerance
Sitting safe ~ in God's palm.

My Body, My Car

Think of your body
As if it were a car...
What would you be ~
Or do you *know* what you are?

A Porsche? BMW?
A race car for draggin'?
A dump truck? A van?
A Ford LTD wagon?

Whatever the style
Of the exterior frame
It's the *motor* that drives
The soul of your name

To take this thought further ~
What if you rust?
Damage invading
Your exterior crust

Well, just as your auto
Goes in for repairs
Some Bondo or Duct Tape
Could restore your flair

Your body is fragile
The engine, your soul
Without its full energy
You're out of control

So don't give your engine
The wrong kind of fuel
Or you may require
A fixing-up tool

73

When you travel down the highway
And you see a troubled car
Pulled over on the shoulder
With its engine hood ajar

Be thankful that *your* engine
Runs great, mile after mile
And as you reach your destination
You can honk your horn and smile

California

Way to the West's
An unusual state
Beaches, sun, wine, and Redwoods...
California is great!

We traveled to visit
Friends in that strange land
But few things regarding
Our trip went as planned

We left snowy Ohio
We flew out to L.A.
When we stepped off the plane
It was like a spring day

We rented a car
Take the freeway? Sure! Swell!
There were six lanes of traffic
All goin' like hell

Ohio has road signs
With numbers connecting
In L.A. it's a new way ~
Roads "to" intersecting

We got *nowhere **fast***
We had not driven far...
Sitting still on the freeway
No idea where we are

Once at our destination
The *visit* was fun
But we drove several hours
For ten minutes of sun........

Red Hair

A boy or a girl?
No more a surprise ~
Ultrasound hides the color
Of the hair and the eyes

When baby comes calling
We all wait to see
The details of life
And who it will be

Once in a while
Something "extra" takes place
You can tell from the look
Upon everyone's face

A redhead appears
What a wonderful find
God has designed them
The gems of our kind

The one unique item
Beyond the red hair
Is the beauty inside
This person so fair

Some come with freckles
Some with dark skin
Green eyes are special
At Christmas they're *"in"*

The redhead's my favorite
A human being jewel
The ruby of people
God ~ and I ~ think they're cool

Jealousy

Is money the object
We all want to find?
The answer to all
The problems of mankind?

I really don't think so ~
It's just *one* of the tools
It *can* be our demise...
Making us greedy fools.

A plan put to paper
Is just merely that
If jealously is the driver
And money's the catch

Be careful what you wish for
And how it is driven
If jealously you're wishing
For gifts to be given

The *essence* of giving
~ Of attaining success ~
And instead of prosperity
You will always have less.

For gifts have great power
They are given away
To lighten the burdens
We carry each day.

Living on a Boat

My cousins live
Aboard a sailboat
Is the dock their front porch?
What is life like, "afloat"?

They seem very happy
As they "sail" through life
In a space ten-by-thirty
Very close, man and wife!

Watch falling stars
And make some wishes
Come and go with the tides
Catch and cook tasty fishes

Do you have a dream?
Could you live it out?
Sure, it can be risky
Without a doubt.

I believe that is *living*
Why are you waiting
For *future* rewards
To be accumulating?

Today is what counts!
Seize the day! Carpe Diem!
Don't waste one more moment!
Embrace your freedom!

The Garden

I do this for God
Tend to the plants
Keeping an order
Knowing at a glance

How to arrange it ~
A bed for their growth
Building the soil
Mike and I, both

Together we work it
This beautiful place
I enjoy the smiles
It brings to one's face

Of course they're the neighbors
Or people who pass
God's given duty
Beyond mowing grass

You know if you have it
It *calls* you in spring
To the dirt ~ to the soil
To tend these living things

It's dancing with nature
It's breathing fresh air
You really don't make them
They're already there

God lets us tend them
Love makes them grow
And if you *get it*
Everyone will know!

79

Itty, wishing he could fly

80

If I Could Fly

I am a cat
I live outside
I only wish
That I could fly

Why? You ask ~
To feed my mind
For birds are my food
Very hard to find

I must stay on the ground
To forage for food
While birds can soar
If in the mood

It's God's perfect plan
Cats meow ~ a bird sings
He gave *me **legs***
Instead of *wings*

I've pondered this difference
While watching birds feed
I sit on my rock
Not hungry for seed

I want *birds* for dinner!
They're such tasty things
Ah! My prayers would be answered
If I only had wings!

Turtles

Turtles are remarkable...
Some well-known "turtle facts"
Are if they live on land or sea
Their *homes* are on their *backs*!

Sometimes I'm like a turtle
My river-home, the shell
I cannot think of any place
That I could love so well

I can retreat inside my shell
Or go explore the shore
Or simply sit and ponder
What my life was like *before* ~

Before we happened by here
And found this place to dwell
They say "Home is where the heart is"
And *my* heart is in this "shell".

82

On the Dock

By the shore of the river
It silently stood
It captured our hearts ~
This patchwork of wood.

Ever so modest
Yet, with great allure
It summons you nearer
For what, you're not sure.

Each season's so different
Mother Nature's clock
Provides timely adventures
Down by the dock.

As you walk down the stairs
To approach water's edge
It's hard to resist
Sitting perched on the ledge.

For some it means fishing
Or you can just sit
And dangle your feet
In the water under it.

It can secure a boat
It sports a great view
Swimmers dive off the side
Kingfishers perch, too.

The structure's so simple
Yet so complex, too.
Simple pleasures await
Those who pursue

A walk on the water
A pause in the sun
A place to relax
When the day's work is done.

Seasons

Spring's an awakening
Gardens reflect
The intricate way
Life and Death intersect

Summer abundant
Garden dirt so warm
Caretaker for God's creations
Enjoying beauty and form

Following summer
Autumn leaves change their hue
Setting landscapes ablaze
Vibrant color renewed

Winter is for renewal
The season of rest
Gardens save energy
Maybe they know best

Pause is required
No electricity
Taking stock of life's bounty
Reflecting seriously

To all things there's a season
Follow your heart
Let go of your fears
It's never too late to start

When They Tell You

We did what we enjoyed, then.
We took them all along ~
The friends of our young children
To camp and sing some songs.

We boated on the water
We taught them all to ski
We never seemed to tire
Because the kids were fun to see.

Because we were committed
To enjoy life ~ every day
Every weekend moment
Was meant for us to play.

Adults that *played* **beside** them
And never told them "no"
Gave them courage to try these new things ~
Helped their confidence to grow.

We thought that this was normal
To include everyone
No matter what their color
Or fear of water fun.

The cost was not an object ~
We took them all for free
To enjoy the pleasure
That *all* children should see.

87

This was fun at its finest
With children all around
Little did we know then
What these kids had found.

Now that we are older
And those children are adults
They have returned to tell us
Of some of the results.

They have come to notice
The difference that we made
Because we loved them equally ~
Whatever their skin shade.

And, if they feared the water
We helped them overcome
By teaching them to swim and ski
And join in all the fun.

And now, they come to visit ~
To pay us compliments...
Hugs of appreciation...
Cherished sentiments.

Thanks to Tom Bonham for introducing me to the river.

To order copies of this book:

Fax this form to: 1-866-436-6866.
Telephone orders: Call 1-419-436-1975
Email orders: leslie@drollenterprises.com

Mail orders: Droll Enterprises –1
              PO Box 641,
              Fostoria, Ohio   44830

Please send _____books @ $14.95 each plus shipping and handling.
I understand that I may return the book for full refund – for any reason, no
questions asked.

BILL TO: SHIP TO:

Name: _____   Name: _____

Address:_____   Address:_____

PO Box/Apt. #_____   PO Box/Apt. #_____

City:_____State:___   City:_____State:____

Zip:_____Telephone:_____   Zip:_____Telephone:_____

Email address:_____

☐ Include an **Angel Gift Card** for an additional $2.00, with the following
message:

_____

_____

_____

Sales Tax: Please add 5.5% for products shipped to Ohio Addresses.
Shipping & handling by air:
US: $4.00 for first book and $2.00 for each additional
International: $9.00 for first book;$5.00 for each additional.

Payment: ☐ check
☐Credit card: ☐Visa   ☐MasterCard
Card number: _____
Name on card:_____ Exp. Date:_____
Signature:_____